A HIPSTER JOKE BOOK
WRITTEN BY SOMEONE YOU'VE PROBABLY NEVER HEARD OF

PRINTED IN THE UNITED STATES OF AMERICA

ISBN-13: 978-0-9848649-0-4

WHY DID THE HIPSTER RESEARCH THE HISTORY OF KITCHEN TABLES?

TO ENSURE HE KNEW EVERYTHING ABOUT COUNTER CULTURE

WHY DOES THE HIPSTER ALWAYS USE THE MICROWAVE?

HE DOESN'T LIKE THE CONVENTIONAL OVEN

WHAT DO YOU CALL A HIPSTER WITH A SPEECH IMPEDIMENT?

MUMBLR

WHY DOES THE HIPSTER DRINK PABST BLUE RIBBON?

BECAUSE NOBODY LIKES IT

WHEN DID THE HIPSTER EAT BREAKFAST?

LAST NIGHT

WHERE DOES THE HIPSTER GO ON FRIDAY NIGHTS?

SOMEPLACE YOU'VE NEVER HEARD OF

WHAT DID THE HIPSTER SAY WHEN HE WAS ASKED OUT TO DINNER?

I ALREADY HAVE PLANS TO HAVE DONE THAT TWO YEARS AGO

WHY DIDN'T THE HIPSTER SHOW UP TO THE PARTY?

HE WAS THERE
TWO DAYS AGO...

BEFORE YOU WERE

WHAT'S THE DIFFERENCE BETWEEN A HIPSTER & A HOBO?

A HOBO DOESN'T TRY TO LOOK LIKE A BUM

WHY IS THE HIPSTER'S FILING CABINET SO MESSY?

HE DOESN'T LIKE TO LABEL THINGS

HOW DID THE HIPSTER BURN HIS MOUTH?

HE DRANK COFFEE BEFORE IT WAS COOL

HOW DID THE HIPSTER SURVIVE THE LOCOMOTIVE CRASH?

HE GOT OFF THE TRAIN BEFORE IT BLEW UP

WHAT WAS THE HIPSTER'S JOB AT THE CLOCK SHOP?

HE FIXED GEARS

WHY DOES THE HIPSTER LOVE TUNNELS?

THEY REMAIN UNDERGROUND

WHY DOESN'T THE HIPSTER LIKE TICKLE ME ELMO?

BECAUSE HE SOLD OUT BACK IN '96

WHY DID THE HIPSTER'S PICTURES END UP ON THE FLOOR?

HE TOOK THE GLASS OUT OF THE FRAMES

WHY DOESN'T THE HIPSTER SWIM IN THE OCEAN?

IT'S TOO MAIN STREAM

WHY DOES THE HIPSTER ONLY LISTEN TO DEAD MUSICIANS?

HE KNOWS THEY
WILL ALWAYS
BE UNDERGROUND

HOW MANY HIPSTERS DOES IT TAKE TO SCREW IN A LIGHTBULB?

SOME OBSCURE NUMBER YOU'VE NEVER HEARD OF

WHY DID
THE HIPSTER
MAKE SURE
HE HAD AN S.T.D.
BEFORE GOING TO
THE DOCTOR?

SO HIS RESULTS WOULDN'T COME BACK NORMAL

WHY DID THE HIPSTER THROW AWAY HIS LAXATIVES?

TO REMAIN IRREGULAR

A HIPSTER'S ACTIONS...

SPEAK LOUDER THAN WORDS YOU CAN'T PRONOUNCE

WHY DID THE HIPSTER INSIST ON SABOTAGING CHARITY ORGANIZATIONS?

HE DIDN'T BELIEVE IN BELIEVE IN DOING ANYTHING FOR THE COMMON GOOD

WHAT IS A HIPSTER'S LEAST FAVORITE FAVORITE BERRY?

A CURRANT

WHAT DID THE HIPSTER SAY TO THE CROWD OF MEAT EATING, MAINSTREAM LISTENING, CONSUMERS?

I "VONNEGUT" AS FAR AWAY FROM YOU AS POSSIBLE

WHAT HOTEL DOES THE HIPSTER REFUSE TO STAY IN?

THE STANDARD

WHY DOES THE HIPSTER LOVE BEING A PARENT?

HE CAN
CONSTANTLY
TELL HIS
KID THAT
HE DID
EVERYTHING
HE'S DOING
30 YEARS
BEFORE HIM

WHY WON'T THE HIPSTER LISTEN TO RAY CHARLES?

HE HAS
RAY-BANS

WHY DOESN'T THE HIPSTER LIKE *TEMPERPEDIC* MATTRESSES?

THEY CONFORM

WHY WON'T THE HIPSTER LISTEN TO HIS PARENTS?

HE ONLY LISTENS TO VINYL

TWO HIPSTERS WALK INTO A BAR YOU'VE NEVER HEARD OF BEFORE...

THE
FIRST
ONE DID IT
BEFORE IT
WAS COOL,
AND THE
SECOND ONE
DID IT
IRONICALLY

WHY DIDN'T ANYONE SHOW UP TO THE HIPSTER'S PARTY?

ONLY HE KNEW WHERE IT WAS

WHY WON'T A HIPSTER USE MAJOR CREDIT CARDS?

THEY'RE ACCEPTED EVERYWHERE

WHY DOESN'T THE HIPSTER NEED TEETH?

HE DOESN'T
BITE ANYTHING

WHY DID THE HIPSTER
MOVE INTO A FLAT
IN FRONT OF TWO
CLOCK TOWERS?

SO HE IS ALWAYS AHEAD OF THE TIMES

A PICTURE A HIPSTER PAINTS...

IS WORTH A THOUSAND WORDS THAT YOU'VE NEVER HEARD OF

WHY DID THE HIPSTER RIP DOWN ALL HIS PICTURES?

SO ALL HIS PHOTOGRAPHY WAS OFF THE WALL

WHY DID THE HIPSTER GET E-COLI?

EVERYTHING HE ATE WAS RARE

WHY WASN'T THE HIPSTER SURPRISED WHEN HE COULDN'T GET INTO THE ZOO?

HE KNEW THAT
ANYTHING
HAVING TO
DO WITH
ANIMAL COLLECTIVE
WOULD SELL OUT

WHY WAS THE HIPSTER EXCITED WHEN HE ACQUIRED AN ILLNESS IN A THIRD WORLD COUNTRY?

HE HAD CAUGHT THE UNCOMMON COLD

WHY WON'T THE HIPSTER SWIM AT THE COMMUNITY POOL?

HE ONLY DIPS IN UNTESTED WATERS

WHY DOESN'T THE HIPSTER WORRY ABOUT GETTING FAT?

HE WAS BORN WITH SKINNY GENES

WHY IS IT IMPOSSIBLE FOR A HIPSTER TO DIE OF STARVATION?

HE CAN ALWAYS EAT THE CHIP ON HIS SHOULDER

WHY DID THE HIPSTER DECIDE TO BE A WOOD SHOP TEACHER?

SO HE IS ALWAYS CUTTING EDGE

WHAT IS THE CAUSE OF MOST HIPSTERS' MENTAL BREAKDOWNS?

NONCONVENTIONAL ANTI-CONSUMERISM POSTMODERN STRESS DISORDER

WHAT DID THE HIPSTER SAY TO THE LADY SELLING MAGAZINES DOOR-TO-DOOR?

NO THANKS...
I ALREADY HÄVE ISSUES

THE END